This book belongs to:

Hello

hello/goodbye

tidy up

play

again

please

I love you

Thank you

sleep

food/eat

milk

water

bib

drink

good night

nappy

bath

teddy

sleep

change

book

hug

baby

mummy

brother

daddy

sister

horse

pig

duck

rabbit

sheep

monkey

fish

goat

dog

COW

cat

bird

animal

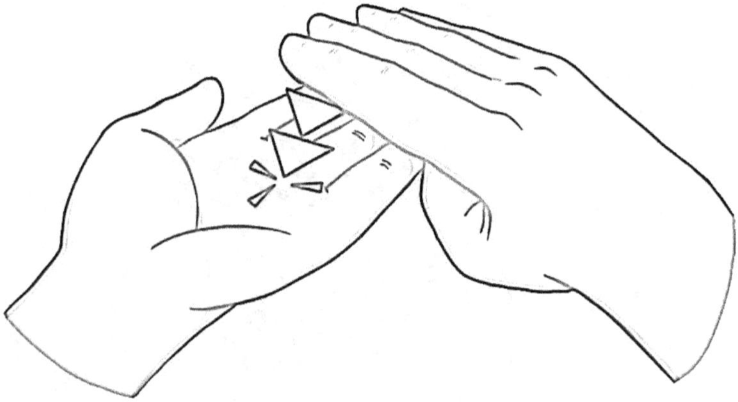

Monday

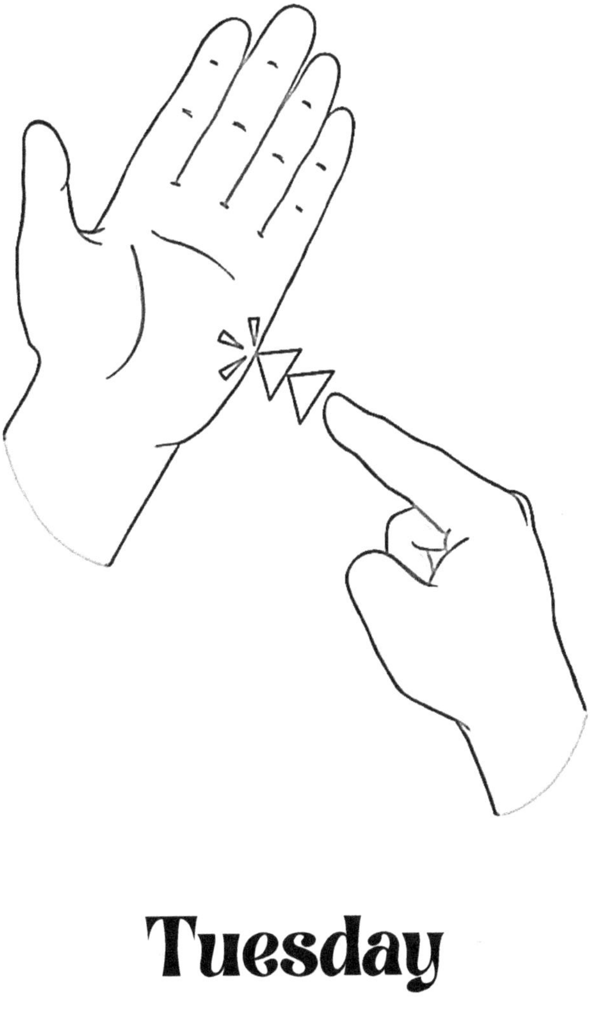

Tuesday

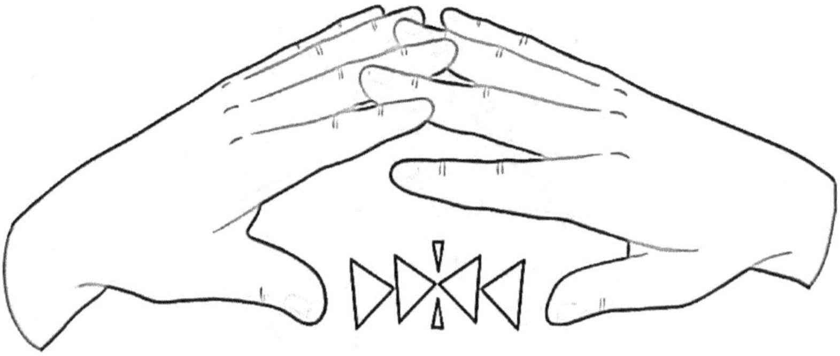

Wednesday

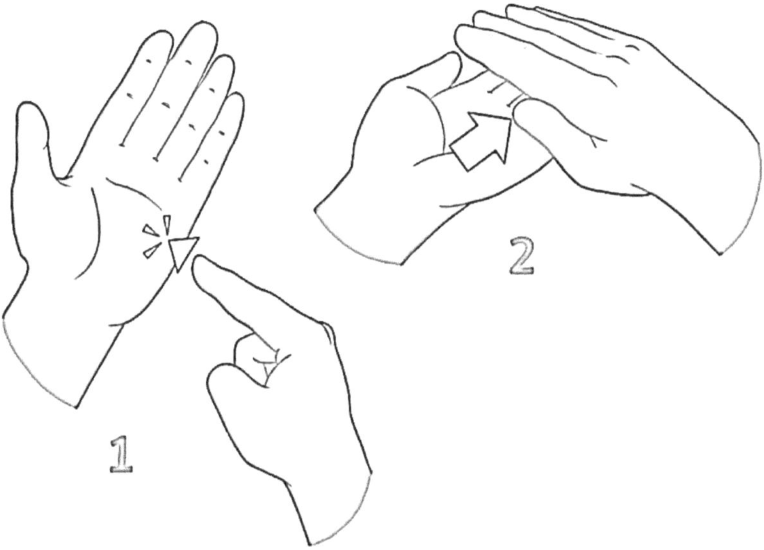

Thursday

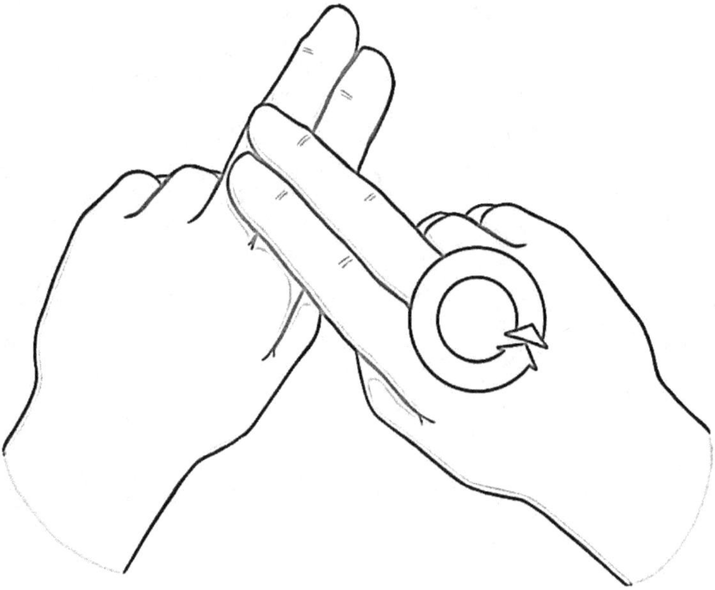

Friday

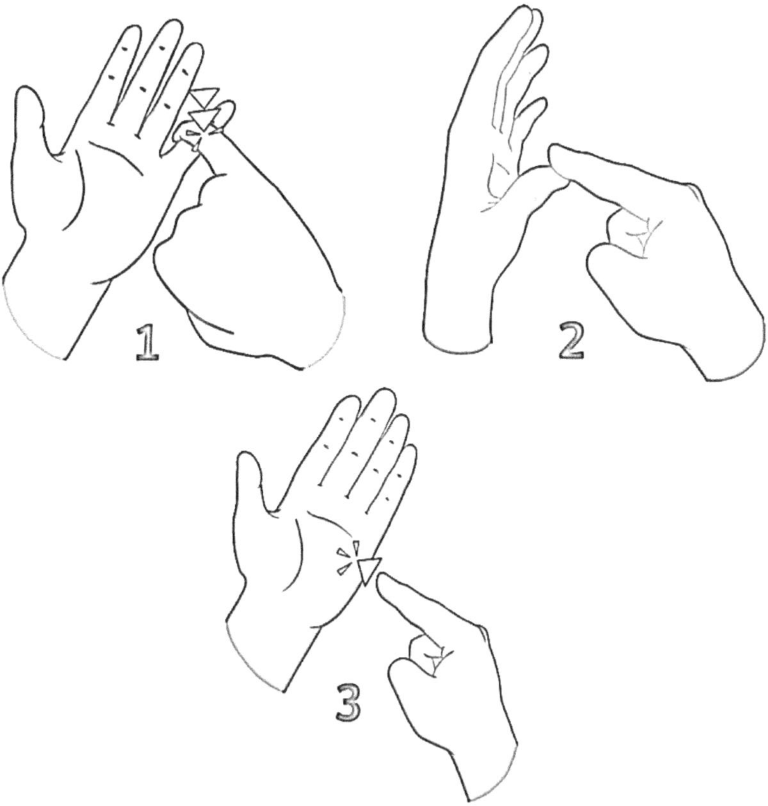

Saturday

Sunday

Thank you!
Please leave a review.

love

www.ingramcontent.com/pod-product-compliance
Lightning Source LLC
LaVergne TN
LVHW020443080526
838202LV00055B/5324
* 9 7 8 5 1 6 5 0 1 1 5 6 6 *